doodling
for
papercrafters

Don't you love opening a new pack of pens or pencils? Sometimes, as I sit with my new pens and half-finished album page, I'm reminded of elementary school and the hopeful feeling a fresh sheet of Manila paper and handful of crayons could produce. I just knew that whatever came of that combination would be especially wonderful, because it would have my personality written all over it. Many other crayoned pictures might be going home at the end of the day, but only one was uniquely me. I'm still putting my mark on many of the things I touch each day—class notes, meeting agendas, take-out menus—and, thanks to Maelynn, I've learned to turn my urge to doodle loose on the scrapbooking page.

Maelynn's collection of doodling ideas is terrific for putting personality on a page and doing it fast. She gives you the whole story on doodling. You'll learn about supplies, doodling, lettering, journaling, and advanced techniques to make your papers into more than just another pretty page.

Give it a whirl.
And get some album extenders. You're going to need them.

Deb Moore
Craft Publications Director

Leisure Arts, Inc.
Little Rock, Arkansas

editorial staff

Sandra Graham Case
Vice President & Editor-in-Chief

Cheryl Nodine Gunnells
Executive Publications Director

Susan White Sullivan
Senior Publications Director

Mark Hawkins
Senior Prepress Director

Debra Nettles
Designer Relations Director

Deb Moore
Craft Publications Director

Rhonda Shelby
Art Publications Director

Katherine Atchison
Photography Manager

Christina Kirkendoll
Technical Editor

Susan McManus Johnson
Associate Editor

Stephanie Johnson
Imaging Technician

Mark R. Potter
Imaging Technician

Lora Puls
Senior Graphic Artist

Jeanne Zaffarano
Graphic Artist

Becky Riddle
Publishing Systems Administrator

Clint Hanson
Publishing Systems Assistant

John Rose
Publishing Systems Assistant

Jason Masters
Contributing Photographer

business staff

Tom Siebenmorgen
Vice President & Chief Operations Officer

Pam Stebbins
Vice President, Sales & Marketing

Margaret Reinold
Sales and Service Director

Jim Dittrich
Vice President, Operations

Rob Thieme
Comptroller, Operations

Stan Raynor
Retail Customer Service Manager

Fred F. Pruss
Print Production Manager

ISBN-13: 978-1-60140-560-9
ISBN-10: 1-60140-560-X

contents

tools

doodles

lettering

journaling

advanced
techniques

inspiration

maelynn cheung,

originally from Hollidaysburg, Pennsylvania now resides in Hoover, Alabama. She has a son, Cory, who is very active and also quite creative. She works full-time in the magazine industry and freelances as a web and graphic designer.

Maelynn teaches scrapbooking classes at Scrapbook Mania in Bessemer, Alabama, and at special events. She specializes in doodling, freestyle, and other technique classes. Maelynn has been published in several magazines and is the design team coordinator for ScrapNfonts as well as a designer for Frances Meyer and Sakura.

For more doodling tips and other scrapbooking and papercrafting ideas, check out Maelynn's blog on her web site at www.ScrapzStudio.com.

maelynn

what is a doodle?

A doodle is any mark or design that you create on your project by hand.
It can be a dotted line or a stick figure drawing. Or maybe an elaborate swirl or hearts that dot the i's in your handwritten journaling. There are no rules here. You may prefer dots over squares or flowers over swirls, but if you like it, that's all that matters.

A plethora of papercrafting products is available to help you duplicate hand-created doodles—rubber stamps, rub-ons, templates, digital brushes, stencils, and more. But, in this book, I'll teach you how to do it yourself and end the fear that overcomes you as you bring a permanent pen close to a pretty page that you've spent so much time on.

so why doodle?

Have you ever thought, "Hmmm...This just needs something.
Not sure what it is, but it just needs something"? That's what I thought when I had an urge to put a little flower on a scrapbook page but didn't want a sticker, paper flower, or other embellishment. I wanted it simpler. It probably would have been fine without it, but something was calling me to get out my pen. I was hesitant at first, but then, I did it and it turned out okay. Not exactly as I had envisioned it, but okay nonetheless.

After this, I was hooked. Now, as I get close to completing a card, layout, or other project, I still get that weird feeling that can only be squelched when I put pen to paper. I've since doodled on many pages, and I've learned lots of lessons along the way. Hopefully, you'll benefit from my experiences through the techniques and tips I share in this book.

You'll learn about different kinds of doodling techniques and designs, what tools are necessary, what tools aren't necessary but are a lot of fun, and even how to easily adjust your handwriting to make it more artsy. I've taught these techniques in my doodling classes, and the students repeatedly comment about how they never realized doodling was so simple.

I hope you feel the same way as you learn from my techniques and the examples contributed by other papercrafters. Have fun learning to doodle!

tools

It's so much fun to add your own personal touch to your creations with doodles. I believe the biggest fear most people have with doodling is the fear of ruining a project they've worked hard to create. There are several tools and techniques to help make doodling almost error-proof. Start with the basic tools; then, add extras as you progress.

the doodler's basic toolkit

sharpened pencil

The most important tool is a pencil. Just a regular, fully-sharpened #2 lead pencil is fine. You can use a pencil directly on most scrapbooking papers to help with the placement and design of your doodling. After tracing over the pencil lines with a pigment pen and allowing the ink to dry, you can erase the pencil without smearing the pigment. Using a pencil may seem like common sense, but my students usually find this tip the most exciting. It makes doodling more approachable.

pencil sharpener

Get an electric sharpener if you don't already have one. Those elementary school twisty sharpeners just don't cut it!

eraser

The second most important item is a good eraser. A pink eraser will do, but a white eraser is the best choice. You can find white erasers at craft stores with the artist pencils. A white eraser won't leave behind eraser smears like some pink erasers do. If you use a pink eraser, test it on scrap paper before using it on your project.

black pigment pens

These are some of the most-used tools in your doodling arsenal. You'll need them in different nib sizes—.005, .01, .05, .08, and brush tip, for example. I use Sakura Pigma Micron pens in the .05 and .08 nib size most often. They can be found with the scrapbooking supplies or fine artist drawing pens. Zig Millennium and Koh-i-Noor are also good pigment pens. Pigment ink is permanent, fade resistant, and archival quality. You can apply it over your pencil marks, and once it dries, you can erase directly over the ink without harming it. You can also use water-based materials (like dye inks or watercolor pencils) over pigment ink without smearing the ink. The brush tip is especially fun for flourishes, but may seem a little tricky to use at first.

colored pens & markers

Zig, American Crafts, and Sakura Soufflé, Glaze, and Gelly Roll are some of my favorite brands of colored pens and markers. For doodling on medium to dark papers, I recommend the Sakura Soufflé pens. They are very opaque and come in terrific colors. Soufflé pens take a few minutes to dry, so don't be discouraged if at first they don't seem to be working properly. Gelly Roll pens are a standard in papercrafting and work very well for doodling. Glaze pens leave a raised texture. Sakura Permapaque pens work on metal, glass, and other slick surfaces. There is a large selection of pens on the market. Try several to see which ones feel the best to you. Being comfortable with your pens is important when doodling.

opaque white pen

The basic doodler's toolkit should also include a truly opaque, white pen. I highly recommend Uni-ball Signo and Sakura Soufflé. Both pens leave a perfectly opaque white line and flow very smoothly. If properly cared for, neither of these pens skip.

storing your pens

When in doubt, store your pens horizontally. Most pigment pens can be stored either upright or horizontally. Pens with a suspended medium such as most gel pens and Soufflé and Glaze pens should be stored horizontally. Try not to drop these types of pens; this may allow air into the medium, which could cause skipping. Paint pens should be stored tip-down once they've been used so the tips don't harden with dried paint.

toolkit extras

colored pencils

Colored pencils are perfect for coloring in doodles or just adding a little color to your project. They leave a softer line than pigment pens which is great when you want to keep the focus elsewhere on the page.

vanishing ink marker

A Vanishing Ink Marker leaves a light line that will disappear after a few days. This gives you time to draw right on your paper and then go over it with your other pens. You can use the marker in place of a pencil if you like. However, if you aren't pleased with your original lines and draw more, the unused lines can be distracting.

french curves

French curves are templates with curved edges to help make the fancy curves and swirls scrapbookers are so fond of. They include anywhere from three curves to a dozen or more. It may take a little practice to get the hang of them, but it's worth it if you have a hard time freehanding pretty swirls. Look for them in craft or artist supply stores with the drafting and drawing supplies.

oh, my darling

Maelynn Cheung Hoover, AL

For **Oh, My Darling**, I used French curves to help me draw pretty flourishes. Then, I cut them out and glued them to the page.

Supplies: Patterned papers, die-cut frame, and definition circle (My Mind's Eye) • Stickers (Collage Press) • Rub-ons (Autumn Leaves and Die Cuts with a View) • Buttons (Foof-a-La) • Pens (Sakura Soufflé)

doodles

lines, borders, & frames

Lines are the basis of many other, more complex doodles. They are also the best way to start if you're learning to doodle for the first time. Lines can be adapted easily into borders and frames, which makes them the most versatile technique.

Here you'll find many types of lines. Some are smooth, light, and airy. Others are jagged and more serious. You can use different pen sizes to create lines of different widths, which can change the effect of the lines.

so cheesy

Sarah Edens Deville, LA

Supplies: Cardstock and patterned papers (Rob & Bob Studio, Die Cuts with a View, The Paper Studio, and Bazzill Basics Paper) • Embroidery floss (DMC) • Ribbons (Dashes, Dots, & Checks) • Stickers, rub-ons, and stamps (Making Memories) • Flower (Prima) • Brads (Miss Elizabeth's) • Fluid chalk (Colorbok) • Pens (Fiskars Gel Pen and American Crafts Slick Writer) • Other: flower button, photo turns, flower sequins, paperclip, and handcut chipboard bracket

☆ **tip** ☆

See how many different line variations you can draw on one sheet of paper. Also, try using a different pen for each one, marking them with the pen name so you can have a visual pen reference for later.

for the longest time when you'd get tickled you'd just wrinkle you face up and make the funniest and cheesiest little face

Take a look at the illustrations and the example projects;
then, try them yourself.

offset lines

• •

Draw a smooth, slightly squiggly line.

Draw another line on top. Don't try to make it perfect!

You can fill in spaces with color, scribbles, or another pattern.

more line doodles

• •

straight line with pointy or rounded "mountains"

straight line with groups of 3 small lines

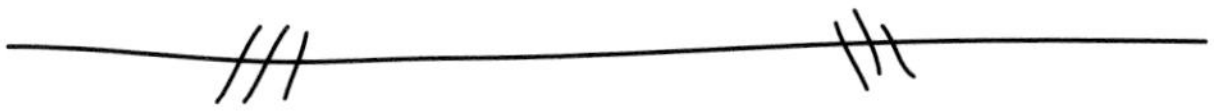

pointy scribbles

straight line with occasional little loops

"EKG" line

or many little loops

scalloped line

straight line accents

toothy line

small squares border

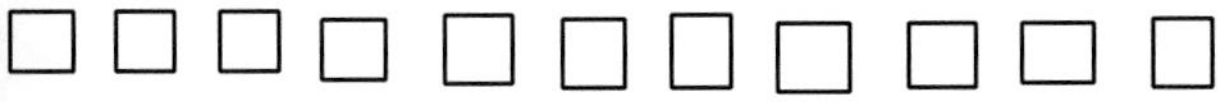

abbreviated or interrupted line

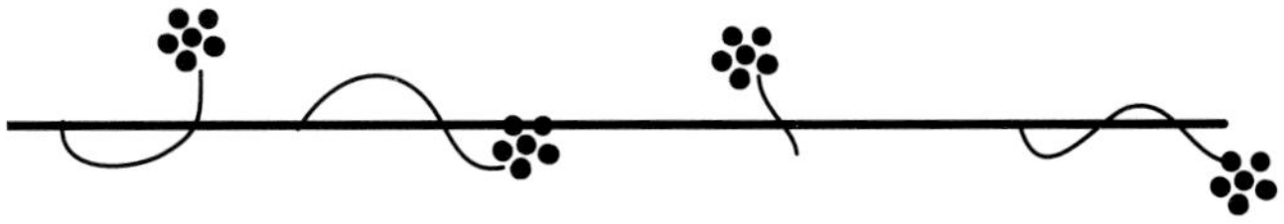

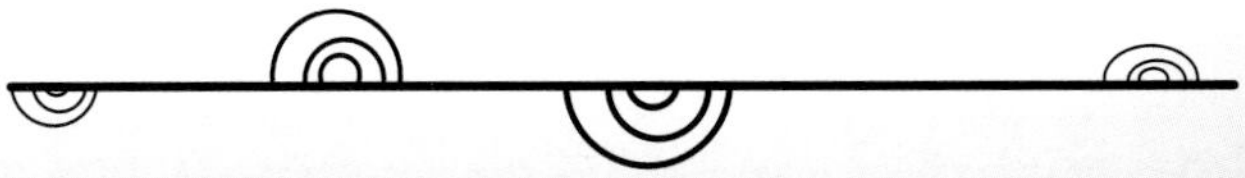

mom board

Maelynn Cheung Hoover, AL

Outlining with a single line is a great technique to start with. On the **Mom Board**, I used a thick line to accentuate the edges of the altered cutting board, the photo, the flowers, and other elements.

Supplies: Patterned papers and die-cut flowers (Fancy Pants Designs) • Pens (Zig Brush Marker and Sharpie) • Buttons (Foof-a-La) • Other: hand-cut letters, adhesive cork, mini clothespins, chipboard, and ribbon

☆ **tip** ☆
Outlining adds e...
emphasis to an o...
so be selective w...
your outlining...

heaven on earth

Maureen Van Dusky Chesterfield, VA

For **Heaven on Earth**, Maureen used light lines along the inside of several of her page elements to help define the angles on the page without being overpowering.

Supplies: Patterned papers, ribbons, and stickers (Basic Grey) • Rhinestone brads (Making Memories) • Flowers (Heidi Swapp) • Buttons (American Crafts) • Pen (Zig)

the hand

Nicole Stark Roy, UT

On **The Hand**, Nicole drew a more abrupt, sketchy outline around the hand. This creates the opposite effect of the light lines on **Heaven on Earth** (page 12) by making the hand more prominent on the page.

Supplies: Cardstock (Bazzill Basics Paper and Provo Craft) • Patterned paper (Carolee's Creations) • Buttons (doodlebug design, inc.) • Stickers (American Crafts) • Pen (Uni-ball Signo)

☆ **tip** ☆
Test your pen on an extra photo to make sure it works on the slick surface.

uncovering t·rex

Maelynn Cheung Hoover, AL

The title letters for **Uncovering T-Rex** didn't have enough punch, so I outlined them with sketchy lines. The lines added to the feel of the page while helping the title stand out.

Supplies: Patterned papers (BasicGrey) • Cardstock (Bazzill Basics Paper) • Stickers (doodlebug design, inc. and Making Memories) • Pen (Sakura Pigma Micron) • Ink pad (Stampabilities) • Ribbon (Offray)

buddies
· · · · · ·

Gina Lideros Elk Grove, CA

Gina drew a few wavy lines around the edges of her **Buddies** layout for a frame effect. She used a fine-point pen to keep it light.

Supplies: Patterned paper, cardstock, and sticker (Making Memories) • Flower (Petaloo) • Clay letters (Li'l Davis Designs) • Pen (Zig Writer) • Corner rounder (Creative Memories)

······ Loopy Lines ······

i've got a crush on you
· · · · · · · · · · · · · ·

Linda Beeson Ventura, CA

For **I've Got a Crush on You**, Linda used a white pen on black cardstock to draw loopy lines around the photo and colorful frame, giving the page a quilted or textile appearance.

Supplies: Cardstock (WorldWin Papers) • Patterned papers (Paper Salon) • Pen (Uni-ball Signo White)

neil and lilly
· · · · · · ·
Kate Siller Worcestershire, England

On **Neil And Lilly,**
Kate drew overlapping
circles of looped lines in
different colors to create
a unique frame.

Supplies: Cardstock, patterned papers, and chipboard
brackets (BasicGrey) • Acrylic paint
(DecoArt) • Pens (Pilot Drawing Pen, Zig, and
Uni Paint Marker)

· · · · · · Zig Zag Lines · · · · · ·

brilliant
· · · · · · ·
Melanie McFarlin Lewisville, TX

Melanie drew white
zigzag stitches around
the paper pieces on her
Brilliant album cover.
This gives the colorful
pieces more punch.

Supplies: Patterned papers and stickers
(KI Memories) • Pen (Sharpie) •
Other: ribbons

······ Scallops & Teeth ······

Scalloped lines remind me of lace edges or the doilies my grandmother kept on her end tables. A variation of the scallop has a rectangular shape (like teeth) instead of being round and soft.

pout
· · · ·

Maelynn Cheung Hoover, AL

I used the toothy version as a border on **Pout**. I used a white pen first, then filled in the teeth with a color that coordinated with the rest of the layout. This helps tie the whole layout together.

Supplies: Patterned papers (Fancy Pants Designs) • Pens (Sakura Gelly Roll, Soufflé, and Uni-ball Signo White) • Other: beads, stickers, craft paints, and colored chalk pencils

my lil piglet
· · · · · · ·

Sarah Edens Deville, LA

The scallops on **My Li'l Piglet** are drawn with heavy lines and only in the corner behind the photo. This draws attention to that area of the layout, so you see the photo first.

Supplies: Cardstock (Die Cuts with a View) • Patterned papers (Wild Asparagus, Scrapbook Wizard, Rob & Bob Studio, and Pebbles Inc.) • Alphabets (Making Memories Mailbox Letters, BasicGrey cardstock stickers, and Pressed Petals Chip Chatter) • Ribbons (Making Memories and Innovative Design) • Decorative tape (Heidi Swapp) • Flower (Prima) • Brad (Making Memories) • Pens (Fiskars Gel Pen and American Crafts Slick Writer) • Pig stamp (Chunky Stamps) • Acrylic paints (Apple Barrel) • Other: sequin flower and rhinestones

my boys
· · · · · · ·

Maelynn Cheung Hoover, AL

On **My Boys**, I broke up the scallops by adding dots in between.

Supplies: Cardstock (Bazzill Basics Paper) • Patterned paper (Crate Paper) • Chipboard (Cosmo Cricket) • Ribbons (Prima) • Pens (Sakura Pigma Micron and Uni-ball Signo) • Distress ink (Tim Holtz) • Other: craft paint

raming

Creating frames with lines is great for drawing attention
to portions of a photo, rather than the entire photo.

crash

Bernadette Henderson Seattle, WA

Bernadette doodled simple frames
with different colors on **Crash** to
draw attention to the parts of
the photo and layout she wanted
to accentuate.

Supplies: Chipboard letter (Heidi Swapp) • Rub-on
(Making Memories) • Stickers (Creative Lettering) • Pens (Sharpie) •
Other: transparency, brads, acrylic paint, and staples

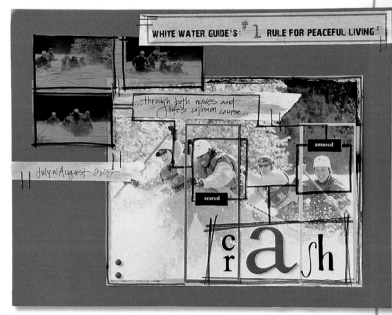

jacques

philippe

Cara Vincens Thionville, France

On **Jacques** and **Philippe**,
Cara framed her images
with black lines, then added
color to the lines to create
instant doodled frames.

Supplies: Mini book and die cuts (Cosmo Cricket) •
Pens (American Crafts, Sakura Permapaque, and
Sharpie Poster Paint) • Stamp (7gypsies) • Buttons
(Dress it Up) • Other: ribbon and staples

dots & circles

Using dots and circles on your pages and projects is another easy and fun technique that will have you doodling in no time. If you can polka-dot, you can doodle. There are a lot of options in this section. The simplest is dotting in a line. Though it may sound one-dimensional, there are several variations of this doodle.

Most likely, as you become more comfortable with certain doodles, you'll use them repeatedly on your projects. Try a few different techniques from the illustrations and example layouts for a fresh approach now and then.

think pink

Andrea Gomoll Brieselang, Germany

On Andrea's **Think Pink** wall art, she used dots and other doodles to accent pre-made flourishes, frames, and a hand-drawn flower.

Supplies: Stickles Glitter Glue (Ranger Industries) • Pens (Zig Millenium) • Chipboard swirls (Maya Road) • Flower brads and acrylic paint (Making Memories) • Flowers (Prima) • Other: dark and light pink felt, ribbon, transparent button, cardstock, and staples

☆ **tip** ☆
If you prefer a perfectly straight line of dots, use a ruler or straight edge as a guide. Test on scrap paper first to make sure the ink doesn't smear when the straight edge is removed.

dots

interconnected circles

large interconnected circles

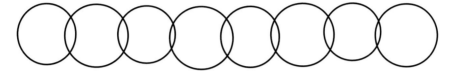

concentric dots and circles

graduated dots

graduated circles

connected "pebbles" with thick lines

connected "pebbles" with thin lines

large scribbled circles

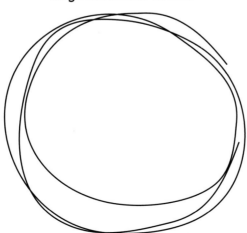

life delights in life

Mireille Divjak Den Helder, Netherlands

Mireille simply dotted borders on the papers and inside the chipboard flourishes on **Life Delights in Life**. She also added dotted bird and butterfly trails.

Supplies: Patterned papers, tags, and chipboard flourishes (Fancy Pants Designs) • Chipboard letters (Heidi Swapp) • Rub-ons (Rhonna Farrer) • Pens (Sakura) • Foam stamps (Making Memories) • Ink (VersaCraft)

peace

Maelynn Cheung Hoover, AL

I used a white Soufflé pen on **Peace** to draw a dotted border. I alternated dot sizes to create a pattern within the lines of dots.

Supplies: Patterned papers (We R Memory Keepers) • Pens (Sakura Soufflé, Pigma Micron, Gelly Roll, and Uni-ball Signo) • Distress ink (Tim Holtz)

cool treats

Debi Gilarde Foxboro, MA

Another easy use for dotting is filling a solid area with a pattern as shown on the top left of **Cool Treats**. Try drawing a freeform shape and fill it in with different types of circles and dots.

Supplies: Cardstock (Bazzill Basics Paper) • Chipboard letters (Heidi Swapp) • Alphabet stickers (Making Memories) • Fabric paper (Michael Miller) • Rub-ons (K&Company) • Pen (Sharpie Poster Paint)

drew

Jeanette Brooks Tuscaloosa, AL

Dots are great for accentuating borders, especially uniquely shaped borders, like the scalloped edge on **Drew**.

Supplies: Patterned papers (BasicGrey) • Cardstock (Bazzill Basics Paper) • Journaling Spots (Heidi Swapp) • Bookplate and brads (Daisy D's) • Letters (Flair Designs) • Pen (Uni-ball Signo White)

love wall hanging

Trisha Peterson Edmond, OK

Dots can be arranged in curved lines or familiar shapes—like hearts or stars. Trisha created dotted swirls and hearts on her **Love Wall Hanging**.

Supplies: Boards and jewels (Junkitz) • Cardstock and cardstock heart (Bazzill Basics Paper) • Patterned papers and stickers (Reminisce) • Flowers (doodlebug design, inc. and Heidi Swapp) • Ribbon (May Arts) • Rings (Karen Foster Design) • Pens (Zig and Uni-ball Signo White)

☆ **tip** ☆
Lightly draw shapes with a pe... first, and then ... on the lines wit... a pen.

absolutely adorable

Tracy Austin San Diego, CA

Tracy drew open circles on **Absolutely Adorable**. Her large circles gently highlight the colorful geometric elements on the patterned paper circles.

Supplies: Patterned papers, stickers, and rub-ons (Polar Bear Press) • Stamps (Autumn Leaves) • Pen (Zig)

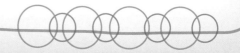

joy of discovery

Melissa Oliveira East Falmouth, MA

On **Joy of Discovery**, Melissa doodled dots and concentric circles around the photo.

play

the joy of DISCOVERY

Supplies: Cardstock (Bazzill Basics Paper) • Patterned paper (Cherry Arte) • Buttons (Foof-a-La) • Ink (Memories) • Pens (Sakura Glaze and Uni-ball Signo) • Stickers (American Crafts) • Flower diecut (Quickutz)

basic swirls

Swirls are easy to spot on layouts. Sometimes, they're just a small accent on a page and sometimes they take up most of the page like a climbing vine (which we'll cover in the next section.) In this section, you'll learn to draw a basic swirl in just a few steps.

The basic swirl has many variations. You can elongate it, shorten it, or only swirl one end. You can keep curling the end in smaller circles like a whirlpool or make it big and broad, as large as you like. Take a look at the examples, give them a try, and see which ones feel good to you. Practicing really pays off with swirls.

lil' miss personality

De Anna Heidmann Whitefish Bay, WI

Supplies: Cardstock (Bazzill Basics Paper) • Patterned papers (Me and My Big Ideas and My Mind's Eye) • Pen (Sharpie) • Sparkle on photo (Adobe Photoshop brush by Anna Aspnes) • Other: brads and buttons

☆ **tip** ☆

If you have trouble drawing the basic swirl, try turning your paper sideways and think of it as a big "S."

24

basic swirl step-by-step

Draw this curved line.
Hint: It looks like an "S" turned on its side.

Add little round hooks at the end of the "S"-curve. These can be circular or oblong, at one end or both.

Draw lines that intersect but run almost parallel with the original curve, leaving space in between.

Fill in the space with pattern or color to give it some dimension.

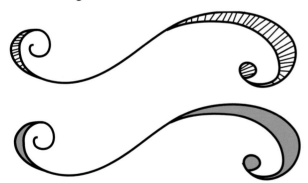

swirl add-ons

Add small loops to the smooth line.

Draw smooth "parallel" lines.

Finish with little dots.

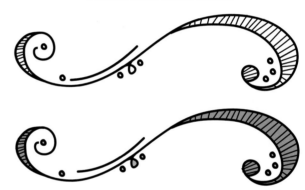

swirl variations

Make the swirl more oblong or extended.

Use long stems with small curls for a more delicate swirl.

25

hank's teeth

Jodie Klatt Mason City, IA

For **Hank's Teeth**, Jodie drew a cute border of basic swirls around the bottom of her altered tin.

Supplies: Tin (Provocraft) • Patterned paper (Piggy Tales) • Acrylic paint (Anita's Acrylic) • Pens (Creative Memories Precious Element) • Rub-ons (American Crafts) • Ribbons (Scrap-Eze and Bobbin Ribbon)

dance

Susan Coish Moncton, NB, Canada

On **Dance**, Susan added the swirls after the large flower to create tendrils that sprout from the flower.

Supplies: Cardstock (Bazzill Basics Paper) • Patterned papers (Three Bugs in a Rug) • Lettering (Heidi Swapp Ghost Letters [traced]) • Pen (Marvy Gel Excel) • Watercolor pencils (Staedtler)

that's the smile
Maelynn Cheung Hoover, AL

I drew basic swirls with a few curly-q's in the middle along strips of paper on two sides of **That's the Smile**. I used a coordinating color that doesn't stand out so much that it takes attention away from the main page elements.

Supplies: Patterned papers (BasicGrey) • Pens (Sharpie) • Other: cardstock and brads

belle
Maelynn Cheung Hoover, AL

On **Belle**, I connected several white swirls together, then traced over them with a thinner black line, adding little flowers and dots along the way.

Supplies: Patterned papers, cardstock stickers, and alphabet stickers (Frances Meyer) • Pens (Sakura Pigma Micron and Sharpie White Paint Marker) • Diecuts (Sizzix)

abbigayle
· · · · · · · ·

Marnie Bushmole Hoffman Estates, IL

Marnie used only the ends of swirls on **Abbigayle**. She used colors that coordinate with her papers.

Supplies: Cardstock (Bazzill Basics Paper) • Patterned papers (Kaleidoscope) • Chipboard letters (Scenic Route Paper Co.) • Oval Die (Sizzix) • Flower punch (Stampin' Up!) • Rhinestones (Westrim) • Pens (Sharpie and Sakura Glaze) • Ink (ColorBox) • Chalk pen (EK Success) • Photo corners (Quickutz)

water baby
· · · · · · · · ·

Shana Dilldine Springtown, TX

On **Water Baby**, Shana drew swirls, filled them in solid, and then bordered them with dots. She added flowers on top of the doodled swirls for a fun look.

Supplies: Cardstock (Bazzill Basics Paper) • Patterned papers (My Mind's Eye) • Flowers (Prima) • Flower punch (EK Success) • Brads (Making Memories) • Buttons (SEI) • Alphabet dies (Sizzix) • Pen (Zig) • Ink (ColorBox)

you are...4

Rita Shimniok Cross Plains, WI

On **You Are...4**, Rita used an opaque pen to add swirls to the large frame. Then, she accented the swirls with jewels, dots, and lines that cross the middles.

Supplies: Cardstock (Bazzill Basics Paper) • Patterned papers (Deja View) •
Chipboard letters and frame (Pressed Petals) • Ribbon (Offray) •
Acrylic slide (Heidi Grace Designs) • Gems (Me and My Big Ideas) •
Stamps (Autumn Leaves) • Chalk (Close to My Heart) •
Ink (ColorBox and Stampendous) • Thread (Coats & Clark) •
Pens (Pentel Milky Gel Roller, Sakura Soufflé, and Zig Writer) •
Other: buttons

vines

Vines seem a bit daunting at first, but they aren't as complicated as they look. This is a doodling technique that most people think they can't accomplish, but they can with a little practice. A vine is simply a long, flowing flourish made of a series of different swirls put together. At first, try drawing them in pieces as shown on the vine step-by-steps. Then, as your vines improve and you feel more comfortable, try drawing one long vine with swirls and loops, and then add in extra curls and accents.

☆ tip ☆

If you are having trouble drawing vines, look at flourish stamps and rub-ons for inspiration.

vine step-by-steps

Vines can be made from basic swirls, curly-q's, and a few accents.

Here, I've drawn basic swirls blue, curly-q's red, and accents green to show you how to break down a large flourish into smaller, less daunting, pieces.

Here is the full vine in black. This would also look great filled in or drawn with color. Give it a try!

Here you can see the line that connects the two groups of pieces together.

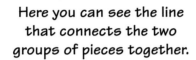

middle of nowhere

Maelynn Cheung Hoover, AL

On **Middle of Nowhere**, I used long, loopy, swirling vines around the main focus—the photo. I lightly drew them in pencil first to figure out the placement, then went over them with a black pen and filled in the spaces with a Soufflé pen.

Supplies: Patterned papers (Kaleidoscope and Wild Asparagus) • Stickers (American Crafts) • Pens (Sakura Soufflé and Pigma Micron) • Other: ink

create

Andrea Wiebe Westbank, BC, Canada

Andrea doodled a tight, curly vine on the right side of **Create**.

Supplies: Patterned papers (Provo Craft) • Cardstock (Bazzill Basics Paper) • Ribbons (Autumn Leaves, Heidi Swapp, Offray, and May Arts) • Photo turns and brads (Autumn Leaves) • Pens (Sakura Micron and Gelly Roll) • Stickers (KI Memories) • Chipboard Diamonds (Heidi Swapp) • Ink (ColorBox)

cd-tin album

Robyn Bedsaul Bel Air, MD

On the **CD-Tin Album**, Robyn drew small vine accents to add a little decoration where space was limited. She used an opaque white pen directly on the photo on the "blessings" page.

Supplies: Tin (Effectuality Inc.) • Cardstock (Bazzill Basics Paper) • Trim, journal block, and sequins (Jenni Bowlin) • Pens (Marvy Uchida Medallion, Sharpie Poster Paint, Zig Millenium, and American Crafts) • Flowers (Prima) • Other: alphabet stamps and buttons

☆ **tip** ☆
Bigger isn't always better! It's easier to start with a small area of doodling and add more later if you think it's needed.

easter

Bridget Farrington Colorado Springs, CO

On **Easter**, Bridget drew a few long stems and then doodled lots of swirled vines off the main stems. She accented them beautifully with color and added tiny leaves.

Supplies: Cardstock (Bazzill Basics Paper) • Patterned papers (Chatterbox) • Pens (Sakura Soufflé and Pigma Micron) • Other: transparent buttons

paradise

Cathy Schellenberg Steinbach, MB, Canada

On **Paradise**, Cathy picked up on the swirly patterned paper and created more prominent swirly vines directly on the paper. She kept them bare with no color to keep the emphasis on the photo.

Supplies: Patterned paper (Around the Block) • Chipboard letters (Scenic Route Paper Co.) • Pen (Uni-ball Signo White)

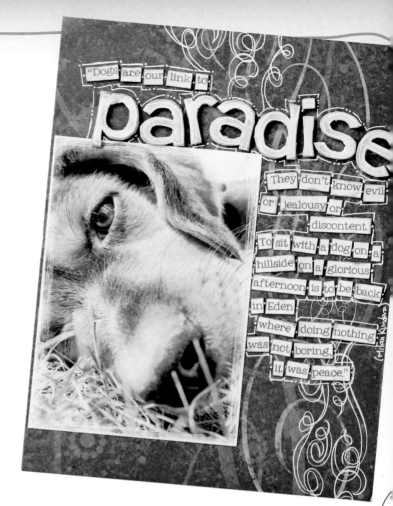

memories

LaTonya Boike Cullman, AL

Overlapping vines and swirls is another fun doodling technique. On **Memories**, the black vines overlap each other in places. Don't overdo this technique; too much can overwhelm the layout.

Supplies: Patterned papers (My Mind's Eye and Cosmo Cricket) • Acetate heart (Heidi Swapp Ghost Shape) • Rhinestones (Heidi Swapp and My Mind's Eye) • Flowers (Prima and other) • Pen (Sakura Gel Pen) • Other: glass buttons

doodle bag

Donna Salazar Irvine, CA

On the **Doodle Bag**, Donna drew vines made of swirls that build off one another. She filled in spaces with a light green pen and drew a few flowers along the vines.

Supplies: Pens (Y & C FabricMate, and Marvy Uchida Brush Tip Fabric Markers) • 3-D fabric paint (Scribbles) • Other: denim bag and bleach

Doodle Bag Recipe
1. Denim bag
2. Clorox bleach & spray bottle
3. Y & C FabricMate black fabric pen
4. Marvy Uchida Brush-tip fabric Markers; Green, Lt. Green, Purple
5. Scribbles 3D paint Shiny: white, black, bright yellow & Glittering Crystal

❀ flowers ❀

Flowers are everywhere! There are paper flowers, rub-on flowers, chipboard flowers, flower stickers, flower diecuts, flower stamps…and flower doodles! Flowers are great doodles to learn because they are so versatile. You can doodle large daisies or tiny posies. Or, you can use some of those wonderful flower products and doodle around them or directly on them to give them your own personal touch.

Refer to the floral illustrations as you practice different flowers, stems, and leaves. Then, check out the examples provided for more inspiration.

happy
Kimberly Archer Gainesville, GA

On **Happy,** Kimberly doodled groups of different-sized white flowers on the dark background paper to complement the bright-colored papers that frame the photo. She didn't completely cover the open space, so the photo remains the primary focus.

Supplies: Cardstock (Bazzill Basics Paper) •
Patterned papers (A2Z Essentials) •
Chipboard letters (Heidi Swapp) •
Pen (Sharpie Poster Paint)

flowers and leaves

For an easy flower, put a dot where you want the center of the flower. Then, starting from the dot, draw a loop out and back to the center. Draw another loop directly across from that petal. Continue around until you've added all the petals you want.

Try the same technique, but use a circle as your center point and make the petals more shallow and wide.

For these flowers, draw a center circle and five small circles or dots for petals. For larger versions of this technique, use a pencil eraser dipped in paint to make dots.

Use a center circle with closely-set dots for petals.

Make them small and add a thin line for a stem.

basic leaf

Try curvier edges.

Or make little leaves and fill them with color.

Draw lines for stems.

Add roughly-drawn flower shapes.

Fill them in with solid black or color(s), if you'd like.

37

girls rule

Maelynn Cheung Hoover, AL

Drawing around flower die-cuts or stickers that you've applied to your page is an easy way to get started with flowers. On **Girls Rule**, I applied several flowers in a semi-circle and then doodled around them with three lines to unify them.

Supplies: Patterned papers and cardstock stickers (KI Memories) • Chipboard alphabets (Pressed Petals) • Markers (Zig) • Dye ink (Stamp Craft)

☆ tip ☆

If the flowers are punch-out diecuts or stickers, it may be easier to draw your borders on the flowers before you remove them from the sheet.

you're beautiful

Lana Bisson Killeen, TX

Lana also used pre-made flowers on **You're Beautiful**. She used a black pen to draw borders inside the edges of some of the paper flowers and added some wispy doodles coming from a couple of the flowers.

Supplies: Cardstock (Bazzill Basics Paper) • Patterned papers (Paper Pizzazz) • Rhinestone brads and clips (Making Memories) • Buttons, glitter, stamps, and markers (Stampin' Up!) • Rhinestone words (Me and My Big Ideas) • Rhinestones (Heidi Swapp) • Paper punches (EK Success) • Pen (Uni-ball) • Trim (Wal-Mart) • Glossy Accents (Ranger Industries) • Other: chipboard scraps

flirt with red

Rita Shimniok Cross Plains, WI

On **Flirt with Red**, Rita used a Soufflé pen to doodle stems and leaves on black paper to coordinate with the patterned paper. She also added red and white dots that work well with the polka-dot ribbon.

Supplies: Cardstock (Bazzill Basics Paper) • Patterned papers, chipboard alphabets, photo corners, frame, and tag (Scenic Route Paper Co.) • Chipboard washer and mini flower (BasicGrey) • Brads (Queen & Co., Karen Foster Design, and Making Memories) • Clear glaze (Mod Podge) • Ribbons (Offray and other) • Pens (Sakura Soufflé and Glaze and Pentel Milky Gell Roller) • Other: flowers

little girls no more

Maelynn Cheung Hoover, AL

On **Little Girls No More**, I connected several layered flowers with a doodled vine that has leaves and curly-q's. This pretty effect joins the flowers together nicely.

Supplies: Cardstock (Bazzill Basics Paper) • Patterned papers (Frances Meyer, Fancy Pants Designs, and My Mind's Eye) • Chipboard (Frances Meyer) • Pens (Sakura Pigma Micron) • Colored pencils and Giaconda pastel pencils (Koh-i-noor) • Other: vellum and buttons

soul sista
· · · · · · ·

Julie Ann Shahin Rochester, NY

Julie Ann doodled flowers, stems, and leaves on **Soul Sista**. Then, she used a paper piercer to punch holes along the lines and hand stitched the design.

Supplies: Cardstock (Bazzill Basics Paper) • Patterned paper (KI Memories) • Pens (Zig) • Hinges, thread, and girlfriends ribbon (Making Memories) • Chipboard letters (Zsiage and Li'l Davis Designs) • Other: staple and fabric strips

☆ **tip** ☆
To cut around close corners and into small spaces, use precision-tip scissors or a craft knife.

crazy girl
· · · · · · ·

Julie Fei-Fan Balzer New York, NY

For a fun, translucent look, Julie doodled flowers and title letters on vellum. Then, she cut them out, and overlapping some flowers, adhered them to her **Crazy Girl** layout.

Supplies: Cardstock (Club Scrap) • Pens (Zig and Sakura Pigma Micron) • Other: patterned paper and vellum

beautiful bug hunter

Sudie Alexander Charleston, SC

Sudie stamped flowers with paint on **Beautiful Bug Hunter**. Then, she used a pencil to doodle more flowers and vines on the page. She went over the pencil lines and around the stamped flowers with a pen and then erased the pencil lines. She also outlined the die-cut butterfly with the pen.

Supplies: Patterned paper and tag (Wild Asparagus) • Cardstock (The Paper Company) • Dies (Sizzix) • Stamps (Heidi Swapp) • Acrylic paint (Making Memories) • Pen (Creating Memories)

wonderful day
heritage
harmony

Kriss Cramer East Fallowfield, PA

Each of Kriss' cards displays a different flower doodling technique. **Wonderful Day** has three dots at the end of each stem, **Heritage** has small blue swirls with a lighter blue beneath them, and **Harmony** has small flower shapes loosely filled in with color. All three have sweeping green strokes in two shades for the stems.

Supplies: Pigment pens, dye ink, alcohol ink, Metallic Mixatives, alcohol blending solution, ink applicator and felt, and gloss paper (Ranger Industries) • Stamps (Hero Arts) • Other: cardstock

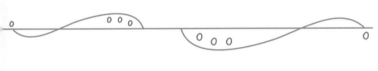

{ accents & extras }

I doodle on almost every scrapbook page or craft I create, and I haven't duplicated my doodles yet. The possibilities are endless when it comes to drawing doodles. Don't stop at swirls, dots, and flowers! Try arrows, hearts, and stars, too!

little red naughty chair

Michelle Cathcart Sugar Grove, PA

Instead of just putting the number 2 on **Little Red Naughty Chair**, Michelle put the numbers 1–9 and then circled the 2 to bring attention to it.

Supplies: Patterned papers (KI Memories and Daisy D's) • File folder, photo turn, and brad (Making Memories) • Chipboard clock (Heidi Swapp) • Embroidery floss (DMC) • Paper clip (Spare Parts) • Stickers (Die Cuts with a View and American Crafts) • Pen (Zig Millenium) • Rub-ons (Junkitz) • Other: buttons

☆ **tip** ☆
Try the same technique with a calendar rubber stamp. Circle a special date, or print the days of the week in black but make a special day a different color so it stands out.

jump

Maelynn Cheung Hoover, AL

On **Jump**, I used swirls and arrows together to add interest to the solid green cardstock. Arrows help direct the eye toward a specific point—
in this case, the photos.

Supplies: Patterned paper (Sassafrass Lass) • Cardstock (Bazzill Basics Paper) • Chipboard brackets (Trace Industries) • Coaster Circles (Gin-X) • Stickers (American Crafts) • Pens (Sakura Soufflé, Sharpie, and Uni-ball Signo White) • Ink (Versacolor)

☆ **tip** ☆

Try doodling on buttons, met embellishments, rib and flowers. Be su test your pens the items first

sisters always

Alison Lockett Knoxville, TN

Doodling on something other than paper is quite fun! On **Sisters Always**, Alison doodled directly onto colorful buttons which works well with the polka-dot flowers and the doodles on the letters.

Supplies: Cardstock (Bazzill Basics Paper) • Patterned papers and stamp (7gypsies) • Ribbons (Offray and Stampin' Up!) • Flowers (Creating Keepsakes, doodlebug design, inc., American Crafts, and Bazzill) • Brads (Creating Keepsakes) • Buttons (Die Cuts with a View) • Chipboard letters (Scenic Route Paper Co. and Heidi Swapp) • Rub-on (EK Success) • Rickrack (doodlebug design, inc.) • Pen (Zig Opaque Writer) • Tabs (Avery)

i remember

Julie Fei-Fan Balzer New York, NY

Doodled stars make great accents. On **I Remember**, Julie combined vellum and patterned paper stars to create a fun swoosh of stars across her layout.

Supplies: Cardstock (Bazzill Basics Paper) • Pen (Zig Writer) • Foam stamps and paint (Memory Makers) • Other: patterned paper and vellum scraps

IT'S FUNNY. I LOOK AT THIS PICTURE AND I DON'T KNOW WHEN IT WAS TAKEN, OR WHERE IT IS. I DON'T REMEMBER THAT YELLOW TANK TOP OR THE LITTLE CAT PIN I'M WEARING. BUT, I DO REMEMBER THAT BAG, VIVIDLY. THAT'S THE BAG I PACKED TO RUN AWAY FROM HOME. I WAS ANGRY AT MY MOTHER + ANNOUNCED THAT I WAS RUNNING AWAY! I THINK SHE PACKED ME A SANDWICH FOR THE TRIP. I GOT AS FAR AS THE CURB IN FRONT OF OUR HOUSE. I CAN STILL REMEMBER SITTING THERE + CRYING, AND WONDERING WHY SHE WASN'T COMING AFTER ME. SO, AFTER A WHILE, I WENT BACK INSIDE THE HOUSE, CONVINCED THAT NO ONE WOULD CARE OR NOTICE IF I VANISHED FOREVER. THAT'S WHERE MY MEMORY FADS. I'M SURE MY MOTHER FOUND A WAY TO COMFORT ME (I NOW KNOW THAT SHE WATCHED ME THROUGH A WINDOW THE WHOLE TIME), BUT MY EMOTIONS ARE ALL TIED UP IN THE SIGHT OF THAT BAG...

I rEmEmBEr

aaron & hank * 2006

* Brubbar is a word invented by Henry just for his baby brother.

i ♥ my brubbar*

brubbar

Jodie Klatt Mason City, IA

Jodie doodled a heart and stars on red paper, cut them out, and adhered them to her **Brubbar** layout. The repetition of this technique gives the accents on the page continuity.

Supplies: Solid and patterned papers (KI Memories) • Stickers (American Crafts and doodlebug design, inc.) • Pens (Zig Millenium and Marvy Artist double-tipped)

rainy day smiles

Maelynn Cheung Hoover, AL

On **Rainy Day Smiles**, I combined arrows with dots and lines to direct the eye around the page from the title, to the journaling, to the photos.

Supplies: Patterned paper (Francis Meyer) • Cardstock (Bazzill Basics Paper) • Pens (Sakura Soufflé and Pigma Micron) • Chalk ink (Colorbok) • Alphabet diecuts (Cricut)

RAiNy dAy Smiles

our very first vacation together. 3 days at the beach. Problem was it poured rain the entire time. Before we left for home, I took you to the beach anyway, rain + all. you still had a ball, even if it was for only 20 minutes.

2002

i love u card

Andrea Wiebe Westbank, BC, Canada

For the **I Love U Card**, Andrea doodled a few hearts on a cardstock rectangle. She cut slits and threaded ribbon behind the hearts. Then, she glued the rectangle to a blank white card.

Supplies: Cardstock (Bazzill Basics Paper) • Pen (Sakura) • Watercolors (Lyra Osiris) • Ribbon (American Crafts)

heart flutter
. . . .

Marilyn McKnight Edmonton, AB, Canada

On **Heart Flutter**, Marilyn used her white pen to doodle butterflies and hearts and then outlined some of them with gold thread.

Supplies: Cardstock (Bazzill Basics Paper) • Patterned papers (Carolee's Creations, Karen Foster Design, and Creative Imaginations) • Pen (Uni-ball Signo) • Other: gold thread and copper heart

just me...kate
. . . .

Kate O'Brien Denham Springs, LA

Do you remember doodling on your notebooks in school like I do? I used lots of colors, swirls, hearts, and arrows on mine. Kate recreated that same fun look on **Just Me...Kate** by using different colors, shapes, and words to doodle around her name. Just for fun, try filling a whole piece of paper without repeating the same doodle!

Supplies: Cardstock (Stampin' Up!) • Patterned paper (The Paper Boutique) • Chipboard letters (Scrapworks) • Pens (Zig) • Ribbons (Making Memories, Fancy Pants Design, and Offray) • Rub-ons (Making Memories and My Mind's Eye) • Gems (Heidi Swapp)

star struck

Kimberly Archer Gainesville, GA

On **Star Struck,**
Kimberly stamped stars directly on the white background and then doodled over and around them. By not covering the entire page with doodles, she kept the photo and title the focus of the layout, but still gave the page a fun look.

☆ **tip** ☆
Stamp designs on your projects and dress up the star images with doodles.

Supplies: Chipboard letters and star stamp (Heidi Swapp) • Ink (ColorBox) • Pens (Zig Millenium and Sharpie) • Other: cardstock

camo guys

Laina Lamb Bay Village, OH

Corner doodles are another fun and easy idea. Laina drew photo corners and added lines of dots inside. Then, she cut them out and attached them to two corners of **Camo Guys.**

☆ **tip** ☆
Corner doodles are perfect for using up scraps. Doodle photo corners on scrap paper, cut them out, and save them for later.

Supplies: Cardstock (Bazzill Basics Paper) • Patterned paper, transparency letters, diecuts, epoxy accents, and number rub-on • (KI Memories) • Cork letters (Joann Scrap Essentials) • Chipboard arrow (Deluxe Designs) • Labels (Dymo) • Staples and acrylic paint (Making Memories) • Stamps (Sassafras Lass) • Ink (ColorBox) • Pens (Sakura Soufflé and Uni-ball Signo White) • Stars (Vintage) • Dog tag (Li'l Davis Designs) • Acetate star (Heidi Swapp Ghost Shapes)

just wow

Kathleen Taylor Kearneysville, WV

Kathleen created lots of impact with the doodles on **Just Wow**. The black squiggly arrows on the red paper really add some punch. The scribbled arrow heads and title letters work well with the layout subject matter.

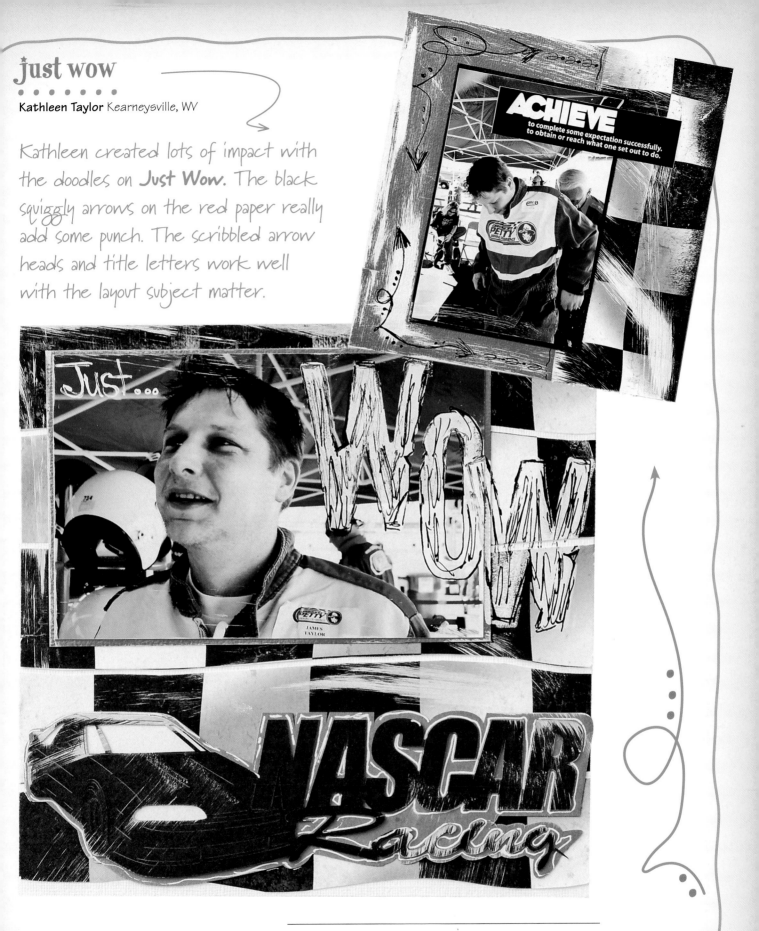

Supplies: Cardstock (Bazzill Basics Paper) • Patterned paper (Karen Foster Design) • Stamps and acrylic paint (Making Memories) • Pens (Pilot Permaball) • Definition (Speed Scrap Design) • Other (Nascar Racing diecut)

lettering

handwriting

Do you like your own handwriting? Most people don't, especially when it comes to adding it to their papercrafts.

I have a few tricks to help you feel more comfortable using your handwriting on your projects. The more you use them, the more natural they will feel.

ALL CAPS

Have you ever seen an engineer's handwriting? It's often in all capital letters, similar to what you see on blueprints, and it looks artsy. Try writing a block of text in all caps. First try small capital letters, then try them larger.

Small Caps

ONCE UPON A TIME, THERE WERE THREE PAPERCRAFTERS.

Large Caps

ONCE UPON A TIME, THERE WERE THREE PAPERCRAFTERS.

Upper & Lower Case Mixed

This technique is a little harder and less natural feeling. You may need to take it slow and think about it a little more at first. Try writing a block of text mixing upper and lower case letters as you write.

Once upon a time there were three papercrafters.

Offsetting the Baseline

This technique feels a little strange at first. You will change the baseline of your letters from one to the next (which means the bottoms of the letters won't line up). It produces a more whimsical look than all capital letters, so it's good for fun, casual scrapbook pages and cards.

Once upon a time there were Three papercrafters.

live, LOVE, and laugh

this kiss

Melissa Oliveira East Falmouth, MA

Melissa offset the baseline of the journaling on **This Kiss**. The unaligned left and right edges of the journaling also contribute to the fun and romantic nature of the page.

this KISS...

symbolizes the beginning of the Rest of my Life... a second chance at Love... a fairy tale come true... hope for a bright future with the Love of my Life.

Supplies: Cardstock (Bazzill Basics Paper) • Patterned paper (BasicGrey) • Buttons (Joann Sew Essentials) • Flowers (Prima) • Ribbon (American Crafts) • Pens (Sakura Soufflé) • Acrylic paint (Making Memories)

OH SO ALIKE!

energetic-silly-true-spirited-loving *creative-cute-impatient-kind-clever-funny-stubborn* IN SO Many many Ways.....

cooper & laina   Aug 06

alike

• • • •

Laina Lamb Bay Village, OH

On **Alike**, Laina used both upper and lower case letters to journal around the blue scalloped paper behind the photo. She wrote with a black pen and filled in spaces inside the letters with colors that coordinate with the layout.

Supplies: Cardstock (Bazzill Basics Paper) • Patterned paper (BasicGrey) • Chipboard letters, crystal brads, acrylic paint, and stamps (Making Memories) • Pens (Zig Millenium, Sakura Glaze, and Uni-ball Signo White) • Buttons (Autumn Leaves) • Ribbon (American Crafts) • Embroidery floss (DMC) • Rub-ons (doodlebug design, inc.) • Rhinestones (Darice)

alphabets

• •

Ribbon Letters

This technique works with both printed and cursive handwriting, though you may want to practice with printed letters first until you get a feel for it.

dear santa

• • • • • • •

Maelynn Cheung Hoover, AL

On **Dear Santa**, I drew white letters, added the ribbons, and then scribbled in the ribbons with white. I also added little blue lines to the left edges of the letters.

Supplies: Patterned papers, rub-ons, chipboard, and diecuts (Fancy Pants Designs) • Pens (Sakura Soufflé and Sharpie) • Other: craft paint

Step 1:
Write your letters as you normally would. The tighter your letters the smaller the ribbons will be.

Step 2:
Draw lines on the left, then right edge of each letter (some of your letters may only have room for a line on one edge). You can draw lines on the inside or outside of each letter, depending on the letter's shape and the amount of space you have on each side.

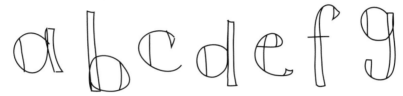

Step 3:
Fill in the ribbons with color or patterns.

a b c d e f g h i
j k l m n o p q
r s t u v w x y z

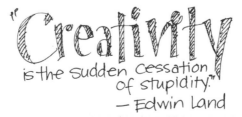

"Creativity is the sudden cessation of stupidity."
— Edwin Land

Swirl Letters

For a fun, whimsical look, try adding swirls
to your handwritten letters.

☆ tip ☆
When writing a lot of
journaling, use swirls
sparingly so it doesn't
become hard to
read.

Step 1:
Write your letters as you normally would.

a b c d e f g

Step 2:
Add small swirls or loops to the ends of each letter.

a b c d e f g h i
j k l m n o p q r
s t u v w x y z

" there is nothing in a caterpillar
that tells you it's going to be
a butterfly."

— BUCKMINSTER FULLER

So be sure when you step. Step with care & great tact & remember that Life's a Great Balancing Act Just never forget to be dexterous & deft and NEVER mix up your right foot with your left -Dr. Seuss

Mariah barefoot in the front yard

WATCH YOUR STEP

on a beautiful spring day.

watch your step

Rosy Schlitzkus Bonney Lake, WA

Rosy not only used pretty swirls on some of the letters on **Watch Your Step**, but she also mixed upper and lower case and wrote her journaling in wavy lines.

Supplies: Patterned paper (Paper Salon) • Cardstock (Bazzill Basics Paper) • Stickers (Junkitz) • Photo corners (Heidi Swapp) • Pen (Uni-ball Signo)

☆ **tip** ☆
To write on wavy lines (or circles or ovals), lightly draw the lines with pencil first. Write your journaling on the lines with pigment pen, allow it to dry, and then erase the pencil.

Outline Letters

When I teach this technique in my classes, I usually hear some "oohs" and "aahs." It's so easy! If you ever need alphabets for a title and just don't have the perfect rub-ons, chipboard letters, or stickers, you can use outline letters.

Step 1:
Leaving space between the letters, write your letters in pencil on cardstock or paper. You can usually write directly on the surface and then erase it. Test a scrap piece first to make sure the eraser doesn't remove the ink from the paper.

Step 2:
Outline your original letters with pencil. Don't forget to do the insides of the letters where needed.

Step 3:
Trace the outlines with a pigment pen.

Step 4:
Once the pigment pen is completely dry, erase directly over the pen to remove the pencil marks.

Step 5:
Cut around each letter, leaving a little space outside the pen.
Remember to cut out the inside areas as needed.
That's it! You have a set of title alphabets!

Lovely

 if

Julie Martinez Orlando, FL

Supplies: Cardstock (Bazzill Basics Paper and WorldWin) • Acrylic paints (Delta) • Stamps (Technique Tuesday and Wal-Mart) • Epoxy circles (Autumn Leaves) • Flowers (Prima) • Brads (Making Memories) • Acetate letters (Heidi Swapp Ghost Letters) • Pens (Sharpie and Uni-ball Signo) • Other: round mirror accents

If you are a dreamer, come in, If you are a dreamer, a wisher, a liar, a hope-er, a pray-er, a magic bean buyer... If you're a pretender, come sit by my fire... For we have some flax-golden tales to spin. Come in! Come in!

"Invitation" - Shel Silverstein

if...

not so sweet sixteen

Maelynn Cheung Hoover, AL

On **Not So Sweet Sixteen**, I quickly sketched black pen lines around my pencil letters before erasing the pencil. The messy lines work well with the layout's subject matter.

Supplies: Patterned papers (BasicGrey) • Cardstock (Bazzill Basics Paper) • Flower (Prima) • Photo turns (7gypsies) • Pens (Zig)

You're a bit of a rebel, even defiant. You're an artist, a musician, an all around good kid. I love you very much, my first nephew. You have a special place in my ♥

chad @ 16

summer 2005

not so sweet Sixteen

he thinks that's cool

Maelynn Cheung Hoover, AL

On **He Thinks That's Cool**, I used the outline letters technique, but made them thicker than usual. The o's ended up touching, so I cut them out together as one piece. I dotted the outline letters with a pen to go with the dots on the rest of the layout.

Supplies: Patterned papers (Scenic Route Paper Co.) • Cardstock (Bazzill Basics Paper) • Stickers (Kelly Panacci) • Distress ink (Tim Holtz) • Pens (Sakura Soufflé and Pigma Micron) • Other: vellum

he thinks that's COOL

his BOXERS are hanging out for ALL to see!

BUT EVERYONE DOES IT!

— CHAD, JUNE 2006

I used to be **TRENDY**. I used to keep up with fashion **FADS**. I remember **JORDACHE** and **CLOGS** and **LEG WARMERS**. Which proves my point. Not every fashion fad is a good one. Don't worry Chad, I'll keep this page for you to ponder **TWENTY YEARS** from now.

oh, brother

Melissa Oliveira East Falmouth, MA

The thin outline title letters on **Oh, Brother** were first drawn on patterned paper and then cut out and applied to the layout.

SPRiNG '06

LAUREN & TYLER

Oh brother

We're strong together as a just reach out & you know i'll be there. In your time of need that's the way its meant to be

family tree

Supplies: Patterned papers (BasicGrey) • Paint (Heidi Swapp, Making Memories, and Ranger Industries) • Buttons (Foof-a-La and Buttons Galore) • Embroidery floss (DMC) • Flowers (Prima) • Pens (Sakura Glaze and American Crafts Precision) • Other: transparency

Other Doodled Alphabets

There are probably hundreds of other ways to create alphabets for your papercrafts. Here are a few others you can start incorporating into your creations now!

you're funny

Kimberly Archer Gainesville, GA

Kimberly used several techniques in the title of **You're Funny**. In addition to the chipboard letters, she traced some of the letters onto the page, filled them in with the pen, and then doodled around them with swirls. This is a great way to finish up a title when you don't have certain letters in your sticker, chipboard, or rub-on stash.

Supplies: Cardstock (Bazzill Basics Paper) •
Chipboard letters and numbers (Heidi Swapp) •
Die-cut flowers (Urban Lily) • Pens (Zig Millenium and Sharpie)

laughter

Becky Thackston Hiram, GA

Becky stamped the title on **Laughter** with foam stamps and acrylic paint and then outlined each letter with a pigment pen to make them stand out.

Supplies: Cardstock (Bazzill Basics Paper) • Patterned paper (Scenic Route Paper Co.) • Stamps and acrylic paint (Making Memories) • Rub-ons (7gypsies) • Distress ink (Tim Holtz) • Pen (Sakura Micron)

u tag my heart

Cathi Beresford Prosper, TX

Cathi traced around chipboard letters for the title of **U Tag My Heart**. Her sketchy lines add movement to the letters.

Supplies: Cardstock (Bazzill Basics Paper) • Chipboard shapes (Making Memories and BasicGrey) • Acrylic paint and eyelets (Making Memories) • Acetate letter (Heidi Swapp Ghost Letters) • Buttons (SEI) • Ribbon/Fibers (BasicGrey) • Pens (Zig)

journaling

Journaling isn't necessarily doodling. But how you journal and what you do to enhance your journaling can certainly be classified as such. Here are a few options:

• Circle a few words in your journaling to make them stand out. Try using colored highlighters to add emphasis.

• Cut each of the words out and adhere them separately.

• Write some words in cursive and print the rest.

• Cut words from magazines or newspapers. (Spray these with archival spray if you feel it's necessary.)

Take a look at the ways the journaling was enhanced on the following layouts.

dirty feet
• • • • •

Maelynn Cheung Hoover, AL

There is a lot to look at on **Dirty Feet**, but if you look at the journaling, you'll see that I used a different color pen and doodles to emphasize certain words. I wrote directly on the page, starting with light pencil marks to make sure the spacing was correct. I erased the pencil after marking with a pigment pen.

Supplies: Cardstock (Bazzill Basics Paper) • Stickers (David Walker) • Pens (Sharpie Paint Marker, Sakura Soufflé, and Zig) • Flowers (Queen & Co.) • Other: walnut ink spray, brown ink pad, and brads

pixie chicks

Tina Werner Otterville, ON, Canada

For **Pixie Chicks**, Tina journaled on a separate piece of paper and then doodled light rectangles around certain words to emphasize them. Then, she cut the words out in strips, put them on her layout, and added even more doodling.

Supplies: Patterned papers (BasicGrey, Scenic Route Paper Co., and Bound + D/termined) • Chipboard letters (Heidi Swapp) • Stickers (Making Memories) • Flowers (Making Memories and Prima) • Pens (Sakura Gelly Roll and Zig) • Other: brads

☆ **tip** ☆
Journaling on a separate piece of paper and then cutting it into strips is a great way to make sure you don't make a mistake on the actual scrapbook page.

These are my girls. My everything. The reason why i do what i do everyday. the ones who make me happy when i am sad and the ones who i want next to me when i am glad. what did i ever do without them when i wasn't a mom. And what did i do with all that time? All i know is my life was incomplete then and they make me so very very happy every single day. I ♥ U 2/06

i ♥ u
• • •
Debi Gilarde Foxboro, MA

Debi journaled in a downward pointed triangle on **I ♥ U** which draws your eye down to the simple heart at the bottom.

Supplies: Cardstock (Bazzill Basics Paper) • Patterned papers and large chipboard heart (BasicGrey) • Flowers (Prima) • Brads and small chipboard heart (Making Memories) • Acetate heart (Heidi Swapp Ghost Shapes) • Stamp (Art Warehouse/Danelle Johnson) • Rickrack (EK Success) • Pen (Sharpie) • Other: buttons

carefree
• • • • •
Cheyenne Clark Rice Lake, WI

Cheyenne created lines on **Carefree** and then softened the line edges a bit by journaling and doodling along them.

Supplies: Patterned paper (KI Memories) • Cardstock (Bazzill Basics Paper) • Chipboard arrow (Magistical Memories) • Acrylic paint (Making Memories) • Pen (American Crafts) • Stickers (Li'l Davis Designs and Artic Frog) • Other: ribbons, buttons, and chipboard daisy

a

Debi Gilarde Foxboro, MA

When you have a photo with empty space, try journaling directly onto the photo like Debi did on **A**. Debi stayed within the edges of the photo, but feel free to run the journaling off the photo onto background.

Supplies: Cardstock (Bazzill Basics Paper) • Patterned papers (BasicGrey) • Button (Foof-a-La) • Stickers (7gypsies and Making Memories) • Chipboard letter (Making Memories) • Chipboard flower (Imagination Project) • Paper pog clip (Autumn Leaves) • Rickrack (Wrights) • Brads (Heidi Swapp) • Embroidery floss (DMC) • Paint (Anita's All Purpose Craft Paint) • Pen (Sharpie Poster Paint)

☆ **tip** ☆
Not all pens write on slick surfaces like glossy photos. Make sure to test your pen first.

i hope

Jennifer Otto Jarrettsville, MD

On **I Hope**, Jennifer wrote her journaling with a black pen and then filled in spaces within the letters with colors to match the rest of the layout. She also doodled around her words, then cut them into strips and applied them to her layout.

Supplies: Cardstock (Bazzill Basics Paper) • Patterned paper and rub-ons (Rhonna Farrar for Autumn Leaves) • Quotation marks (Cricut) • Distress ink (Tim Holtz) • Pens (Uni-ball Signo White and Zig Writer)

advanced techniques

paisleys

There are no limits to what you can do with your newfound doodling techniques. Follow the illustrations and try your hand at doodled paisleys.

mine all mine

Maelynn Cheung Hoover, AL

I accented the title of **Mine All Mine** with a doodled paisley.

Supplies: Cardstock (Bazzill Basics Paper) • Stickers (American Crafts) • Pens (Sakura Soufflé and Pigma Micron) • Other: colored pencils

1 Draw a teardrop with a droopy tip.

2 Draw another inside the first.

3 Draw fun scallops around the outside...

4 and around the inside teardrop.

5 Now, add little open circles to the inside of the scallops.

6 Fill in the inside of the large teardrop with something.

7 Fill in the inside of the small teardrop with something.

8 Add dots at the bumps of the outside scallops.

9 Color it in! FUN! FUN! FUN!

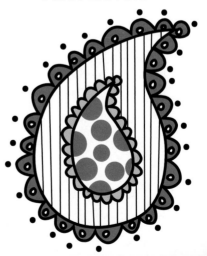

Paisley Options

- Fill a basic paisley with solid colors.

- Use a white pen for the lines and dots.

- Use a little color with black and white pens.

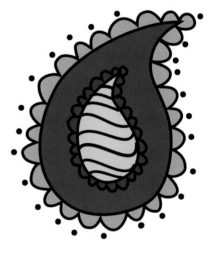

- Use gradated filling...

- or polka dots.

- Use coordinating colors to create a mood or feeling.

- Nest basic paisleys.

- Use funky outlines instead of smooth lines.

- Put several together to make a paisley flower.

Add a loop at the tip.

Add small teardrop accents around the tip.

Fill the entire center with shapes.

Instead of scallops, use another shape around the edges.

Make skinny, elongated paisleys.

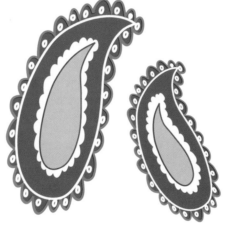

mom's kitchen wall hanging

Maelynn Cheung Hoover, AL

Supplies: Papier-mâché wall hanging (Michaels) •
Cardstock (Die Cuts with a View) • Pens (Sakura Soufflé,
Glaze, Moonlight, and Pigma Micron) • Rub-ons (American Crafts) •
Ribbons (Offray) • Clips (Oriental Trading Co.) • Other: craft paint

cut-out swirls

Doodle swirls or flourishes on cardstock or paper,
cut them out, and adhere them to your project.

ballet

Becky Heisler Waupaca, WI

On **Ballet**, Becky attached cut-out swirls beneath
a flower. It's a really delicate effect that
adds great dimension.

Supplies: Cardstock (Bazzill Basics Paper) • Patterned papers and letters
(Sassafrass Lass) • Chipboard (Heidi Swapp) • Digital Elements (Shabby Princess) •
Pens (Uni-ball Signo and Sakura Gelly Roll) • Colored pencil (Stampin' Up!) •
Ink (Stampabilites) • Other: ribbon

doodled shapes & whimsy

This technique is actually quite old. It dates back many years to when angel wings and crowns were first added into collage and sculpture. It's been adopted recently by papercrafters and scrapbookers to add a bit of whimsy to their work.

sparky

Angela Daniels Reno, NV

Supplies: Patterned papers (BasicGrey) • Chipboard letters (Li'l Davis Designs) • Rhinestone stars (Do-Jiggies by Papyrus) • Pens (Uni-ball Black and Signo White)

invitation

Davinie Fiero Redmond, OR

Supplies: Cardstock (Bazzill Basics Paper) • Patterned papers (Karen Foster Design) • Stickers (Making Memories) • Pen (Zig)

On Angela's **Sparky** layout and Davinie's **Invitation**, they both doodled different styles of crowns and added them to their creations. Draw a crown, angel wings, purse, or eyeglasses; color your design in if you prefer, and then cut it out. Don't even worry about coloring outside the lines. No rules here!

73

trimming doodles for frames

beach bottom

Cathi Beresford Prosper, TX

Cathi used a technique that incorporates her doodling into the structure of her **Beach Bottom** page. To help frame the photo, she cut along the tops of some of her doodled curly-q's and then tucked the photo behind them.

Supplies: Cardstock (Bazzill Basics Paper) • Rickrack (Prima) • Tag (Scrapworks) • Buttons (Foof-a-La) • Pens (Zig Writer)

outlining & filling in flourishes

glamour girl

Corinne Delis Alkmaar, Noord-Holland, Netherlands

On **Glamour Girl**, the blue flourishes outlined in black create a dramatic effect. Corinne continued this technique down the right edge of her page and even atop the photograph.

My sister is definitely a glamour girl, always has been, always will be. She loves clothes and has lots of them. She makes sure she always has matching accessories, and with accessories I mean the whole kabam: Shoes, purses, belts, bandana's, hats and most of all matching Bling Bling!

And what else does a glamour girl like? Attention with a capital A. She was a dancer in a well know group who toured around the world and was on TV in different shows. How should I put this: she loves the camera and the camera loves her. She has all the men at her feet and she knows it.

This is my sister, the glamour girl, and even though we are worlds apart, she holds a special place in my heart.

Supplies: Cardstock (Bazzill Basics Paper) • Patterned paper (Christina Cole) • Rhinestones (Hema) • Foam stamps (Making Memories and Heidi Swapp) • Ink (Agient Page) • Pens (Mitshubishi and Pentel)

freestylin'

you were meant 4 me

Tracy Austin San Diego, CA

For **You Were Meant 4 Me**, Tracy squeezed paint in large circles onto three sheets of patterned paper. Once the paint dried, she cut the paper into four sections and pieced them together. The paper warped at first, but flattened once the paint dried.

Supplies: Patterned paper and stickers (Polar Bear Press) • Acrylic letters (KI Memories) • Paint (Delta Ceramcoat)

life

Jenifer Ashby Chesterfield, VA

Sometimes you may want a more freely-styled look. Jenifer swirled, dotted, and doodled in several places on her **Life** layout. The different doodle styles and techniques give the layout a more spontaneous look.

Supplies: Patterned paper (Die Cuts with a View) • Stamps (K&Company, Inkadinkado, Making Memories, and Tracy Moore) • Distress ink (Tim Holtz) • Brads (Making Memories) • Tag Punch (McGill) • Other: Acrylic paint

machine-stitched doodles

hi tuh-tle…i love you

Tracy Austin San Diego, CA

Tracy machine-stitched swirly lines and a heart on **Hi Tuh-Tle...I Love You**.

Supplies: Patterned papers, stickers, and alphabet kit (Polar Bear Press) • Pen (Zig)

faux stitching

You've probably seen rub-ons that resemble machine stitching. You can doodle dashed lines and X's to create the same look.

single stitches

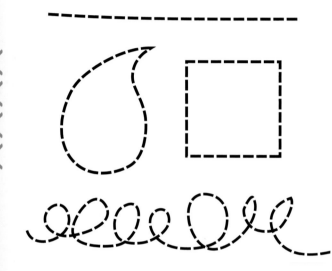

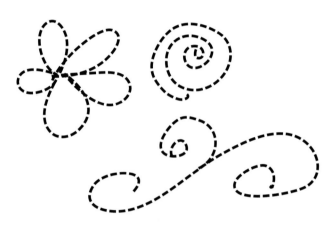

double stitches

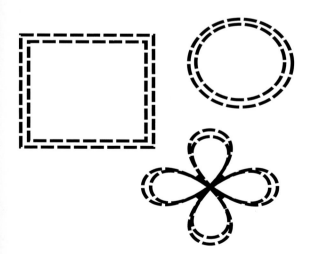

cross stitch

slant stitch

thinking of you card
· · · · · · · · · · · ·

Maelynn Cheung Hoover, AL

On **Thinking of You**, I doodled dashed lines around the card, letters, and other elements to resemble stitching. I added another color next to the black stitches to add dimension.

☆ **tip** ☆
Need faux stitch ideas? Go through your closet and look at some of the stitching on your clothes.

Supplies: Patterned paper (BasicGrey) • Ribbon (Offray) • Pens (Sharpie) • Dye ink (Stampabilities) • Other: cardstock, button, embroidery floss, and brad

inspiration

The great thing about doodling is that there really is no right or wrong way to do it. It allows you to add your own unique touch to your creations that no one else can duplicate exactly. Use this book as a guide to get you started, and with time, your own personality will begin to show through your doodles.

Here are more wonderful creations with doodles of all sorts. I am inspired by all different styles of doodling and papercrafting. I hope you enjoy these, too.

1st born
Emeline Seet Singapore

Supplies: Cardstock and patterned paper (K&Company) • Chipboard swirl (Fancy Pants Design) • Paint (Making Memories) • Flowers (Prima) • Brads (Imaginesce and Queen & Co.) • Chipboard letters (Queen & Co.) • Rhinestones (Heidi Swapp Bling) • Pens (Sakura Glaze) • Other: lace, buttons, and rickrack

me and my dad

. . . .

Casey Rae Foree Fort Worth, TX

Supplies: Cardstock (Die Cuts with a View) •
Stickers (Joann Scrap Essentials) •
Pen (Sharpie)

silly sisters

. . . .

Maelynn Cheung Hoover, AL

Supplies: Patterned papers and rub-ons
(Frances Meyer) • Stickers (American Crafts and
Creative Imaginations) • Pens (Uni-ball Signo)

sassiness
· · · · ·
Linda Peterson Rochester, MI

Supplies: Patterned paper, ribbon, chipboard flower and letter, and tags (We R Memory Keepers) • Pen (Sakura Gelly Roll)

Sassiness is Happiness

S SHANNON

CHIC

IT'S ALL IN THE {eyes}

Nino and Alison have always had such a special bond. In all honesty I have, at times felt a little jealous of their relationship, and then I remind myself of my special bond with my dad. I'm no longer jealous, just happy for them! photo taken Aug 2005 in N.H.

in the eyes
· · · · · · ·
Debi Gilarde Foxboro, MA

Supplies: Cardstock (Die Cuts with a View) • Patterned paper (Rhonna Farrer) • Chipboard hearts and letters (Heidi Swapp) • Acrylic heart (Heidi Grace Designs) • Alphabet stamps (PSX) • Tag (7gypsies) • Pen (Sharpie) • Other: heart stamp

i love that Sommer has always called Emee 'sis ♥

SIS

sis

Staci Compher Carleton, MI

Supplies: Cardstock (Bazzill Basics Paper) • Patterned papers (Urban Lily, Cloud 9 Design, and American Crafts) • Stickers and rub-ons (Heidi Swapp) • Ribbon (Making Memories) • Pens (Zig)

naturally...

Bernadette Henderson Seattle, WA

Supplies: Patterned papers (Rusty Pickle) • Stickers (SEI and EK Success) • Chipboard glitter heart (Heidi Grace Designs) • Pens (Sharpie and Crayola) • Other: cardstock, buttons, and jute twine ribbon

It's so nice to see Edward and Lynda so happy after having their first baby, Tyler. When they first got married, Edward didn't want any children, but I think now he understands the joy fatherhood brings and couldn't be happier.

happy

together

happy together

Charrie Shockey Ardmore, OK

Supplies: Patterned paper (Fancy Pants Design) • Chipboard words (EK Success) • Flower (Prima) • Button (K&Company) • Trim (Wrights) • Brads (Making Memories) • Pen (Zig Writer) • Other: cardstock

zoom

Tina Werner Otterville, ON, Canada

Supplies: Cardstock (Bazzill Basics Paper) • Patterned paper (BasicGrey) • Stickers (American Crafts) • Stamps (Stampin' Up!) • Label (Dymo) • Pens (Zig and Uni-ball Signo White) • Other: buttons

ZOOM ZOOM zoom

went Sophie on the plasma car. Definitely the highlight of our trip to the Children's Museum

you hold the key to my heart

I love you hugs & kisses

I love you more today than yesterday but less than I will tomorrow

Look at US! We have been together for 13 years and we are still goin' strong! We made it through dental school, college & high school together! We got married! We had a beautiful baby boy together! Those are only the highlights! We've come a long way baby! I can't wait to see where we go next! I love you! Eric & April 2006

US

us

April Massad Edmond, OK

Supplies: Cardstock (Bazzill Basics Paper) •
Patterned papers, stickers, rub-ons, and letters
(Three Bugs in a Rug) • Pen (Zig Writer) •
Ink (Stampcraft)

laugh giggle

Staci Compher Carleton, MI

Supplies: Cardstock (Bazzill Basics Paper) •
Patterned paper (My Mind's Eye) •
Chipboard stickers (Heidi Swapp) •
Pens (Zig)

Laugh

giggle

June 2006 • Sommer & Destiny ACTING S

famous last words

Rebecca Hilleary *Charlotte, MI*

Supplies: Patterned cardstock and papers (Chatterbox) •
Rub-ons (KI Memories) • Eyelets (WE R Memory Keepers) •
Ribbon (Oriental Trading Co.) • Chipboard letters (Heidi Swapp) •
Acrylic paint (Making Memories) • Pen (Zig) •
Other: manila file folder

famous LAST WORDS

you have a bunch of them. Around here, you're famous for getting in the last word. It's just in your nature to argue ...and to never be wrong. That = a daily famous last word.

Sebastian...5 yrs

so smart

birthday boy paper bag album

Maelynn Cheung Hoover, AL

Supplies: Cardstock (Die Cuts with a View) • Pens (Uniball Signo, Sakura Glaze, and Moonlight) • Birthday circles (ScrapNFonts Doodlebats) • Other: ribbons and rings

joy mini album

Melissa Oliveira East Falmouth, MA

Supplies: Patterned papers (BasicGrey and Scenic Route Paper Co.) • Rub-ons (Making Memories and KI Memories) • Brads (Queen & Co. and Making Memories) • Flowers (Prima) • Paint (Making Memories) • Pens (Uni-ball Signo and Sakura Glaze) • Ink (Memories) • Other: foam stamp, ribbon, and transparent metal-rimmed tag

just because gift bag

Maelynn Cheung Hoover, AL

Supplies: Bag (Paper Reflections) • Cardstock (Die Cuts with a View) • Patterned paper (Chatterbox) • Pens (Sakura Soufflé and Sharpie)

just because...

Thank You

thank you card

Maelynn Cheung Hoover, AL

Supplies: Cardstock (Die Cuts with a View) • Pens (Sakura Soufflé Pigma Micron, Moonlight, and Uni-ball Signo White) • Adhesive (Zots 3-D)

this makes me happy

Melanie McFarlin Lewisville, TX

Supplies: Patterned papers (BasicGrey) • Stickers (KI Memories and Making Memories) • Pen (Zig) • Other: cardstock

★imperfection★

Maelynn Cheung Hoover, AL

Supplies: Patterned papers (A2Z Essentials) • Die-cut alphabets (Cricut) • Distress ink (Tim Holtz) • Pens (Sakura Soufflé, Pigma Micron, and Uni-ball Signo) • Other: chalk

pens, pencils, and paper

Maelynn Cheung Hoover, AL

Supplies: Cardstock (Die Cuts with a View) •
Pens (Sakura Permapaque, Soufflé, Moonlight,
and Pigma Micron)

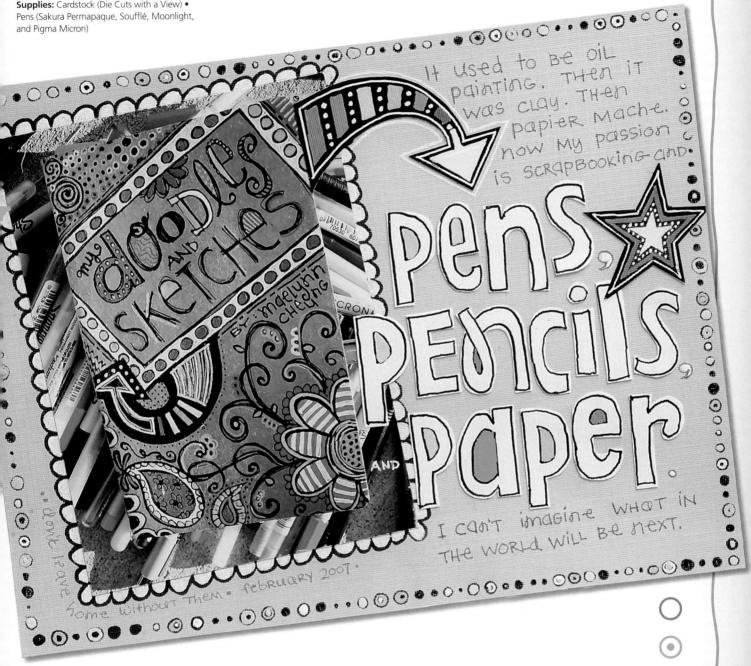

It used to be oil painting. Then it was clay. Then papier mache. Now my passion is scrapbooking and:

pens, pencils, paper

I can't imagine what in the world will be next.

doodles and sketches

by: maelynn cheung

don't leave home without them • february 2007 •

amber's box of little secrets

Mireille Divjak Den Helder, Netherlands

Supplies: Memory Hide A Way (Carolee's Creations) • Ribbons, ribbon slides, frames, and chipboard shapes (Maya Road) • Paint (Making Memories and Aleene's) • Brads (Junkitz) • Pens (Sakura)

stay little

Jenney McAnnally Morris, AL

Supplies: Cardstock (Bazzill Basics Paper and other) • Patterned papers (Scenic Route Paper Co.) • Stickers (Li'l Davis Designs) • Brads (Queen & Co.) • Distress ink (Ranger Industries) • Pens (Zig and Uni-ball Signo White) • Other: photo corners

stay little

green, navy, and gray striped shirt with green outfit

red fluffy pajamas

flannel shirt, corduroy pants, and train sweater

You are growing too fast. We are so busy with daily business that I fail to notice you growing before my eyes. It is when I put away clothes you've outgrown that I realize how big my baby boy is. I love to buy you new outfits and it always breaks my heart a little to pack that same outfit away when you're too big to wear it. It is when I'm staring at a pile of shirts, pants, jackets, and pajamas you've outgrown when I just want my sweet baby boy to STAY LITTLE.

June 2006

love

April Massad Edmond, OK

Supplies: Cardstock (Bazzill Basics Paper) • Patterned papers (Three Bugs in a Rug) • Stamps (Heidi Swapp, Technique Tuesday, and Cherry Arte) • Brads (The Paper Studio) • Heart punch (EK Success) • Pens (Zig and Uni-ball Signo White) • Ink (Stampcraft)

with love

Gina Lideros Elk Grove, CA

Supplies: Cardstock (Bazzill Basics Paper) • Patterned papers (Bo Bunny Press) • Buttons (Making Memories) • Ribbon (May Arts) • Pen (Fiskars) • Other: tag

my guiding star

Nicole Stark Roy, UT

Supplies: Cardstock (Bazzill Basics Paper) • Patterned paper (Scenic Route Paper Co.) • Chipboard stars and letters, plastic letters, and star rub-ons (Heidi Swapp) • Stickers (Making Memories) • Rhinestone star, bookplate, and sequins (Jenni Bowlin Studio) • Paint (Making Memories and Li'l Davis Designs) • Photo corner (QuicKutz) • Pen (Uni-ball Signo)

Within the layout:

my GUIDING ★ **STAR**

Sweetheart you are amazing! Here are just a few reasons why I love you as much as I do . . .

You are continually patient with me. I'm sorry sweetheart for all I've put you through the past year. It hasn't been easy I'm sure. Thanks so much for putting up with the constant mood swings and the ups and downs. Constantly reminding me what we have to look forward to in the eternities together.

You are amazingly sweet and sensitive to my needs. You always know when I need to talk and when you need to push me just a little more to get something out. You've taught me how to communicate and how to express myself. It was a tough job (I know I wouldn't want to deal with me!) but you really rose to the challenge.

Brandon you are an amazing daddy! I love watching you and Wes play. You are doing such a great job showing him how to be a guy. It melts my heart seeing you interact together and realize that this is what I always wanted.

There are so many more things I could list, but just know this you - I love you! You are an amazing husband and daddy and I will forever be grateful for that wonderful day in 2000 when we were made husband and wife. You are my strength and my guide.

18 degrees

Maelynn Cheung Hoover, AL

Supplies: Cardstock (Die Cuts with a View) •
Pens (Sharpie, Sakura Soufflé, and Permapaque) •
Stickers (American Crafts) • Stamps (Autumn Leaves) •
Distress ink (Tim Holtz) • Pigment ink (Stampabilities) •
Green gel paint (Plaid) • Other: white craft paint

the great hunt

Kimberly Archer Gainesville, GA

Supplies: Cardstock (Bazzill Basics Paper) •
Patterned paper (A2Z Essentials) •
Chipboard letters (Heidi Swapp) •
Pens (Sharpie Poster Paint)

froggy BuTT

This was your first time swimming in the pool, and you took right to the water. Kicking like a froggy.

froggy butt

Sarah Edens Deville, LA

Supplies: Cardstock (Bazzill Basics Paper) • Patterned papers (Scrapbook Wizard and K&Company) • Stickers (Making Memories) • Pens (Fiskars and American Crafts Slick Writer) • Rhinestones (Darice) • Ribbon (Making Memories and other) • Flower cut-outs (from a school folder from Wal-Mart) • Other: button